LA-3B

Fun With Letters

D1469234

Author

Clinton S. Hackney

Contributing Authors

Pamela J. Farris
Janice T. Jones
Linda Leonard Lamme

Zaner-Bloser, Inc., P.O. Box 16764, Columbus, Ohio 43216-6764   1-800-421-3018

Developed by Kirchoff/Wohlberg, Inc., in cooperation with Zaner-Bloser Publishers

Printed in the United States of America

01 02 WC 5

Credits

Art: Gloria Elliott: 1–3, 12, 14, 16–17, 19, 21–23; Tom Leonard: 6; Daniel Moreton: 9; Diane Paterson: 13, 16, 18, 24–32; Will Sweeney: 14–15

Photos: John Lei/OPC: 5; Stephen Ogilvy: 4, 6; Jeffry Myers/FPG International, *Children Coloring in Kindergarten*

CONTENTS

New Zaner-Bloser Handwriting 4

Continuous-Stroke Manuscript Alphabet 6

Vertical vs. Slanted Manuscript 8

Emergent Writers 9

Growing Up Writing 10

Getting Started 12

My ABC Book 13

Naming Letters A–Z 14

Learning Basic Strokes 16

My Alphabet Museum 18

Naming and Writing Letter Pairs 19

Naming and Writing Numerals 22

Me, Myself, and I 23

Fun and Games 24

Letter Recognition 24

Phonics Connection 30

Handwriting Strokes 31

You already know handwriting is important.
Now take a look at...

NEW SIMPLIFIED

Zaner-Bloser Handwriting

Easier to read! Easier to write! Easier to teach!

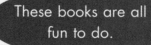

These books are all fun to do.

A **Poster/Wall Chart Super Pak**
includes Handwriting Positions Wall Chart, Keys to Legibility Wall Chart, Alphabet Wall Chart, Simplified Stroke Descriptions, and a Portfolio Assessment Guide

B **Parent Brochure**

C **Kindergarten Round-Up**

D **Pignic Alphabet Book**

E **From Anne to Zach Alphabet Book**

F **Dry Erase Write-On Cards**

G **My ABC Journal**

H **Story Journals**

I **Sentence Strips**

J **Letter Cards**

K **Read, Write, and Color Alphabet Mat**

L **Practice Masters**

M **Illustrated Alphabet Strips**

N **Alphabet Wall Strips**

O **Manuscript Kin-Tac Cards**

P **Fun With Handwriting**

Q **Manuscript/Cursive Fonts**

R **Write-On, Wipe-Off Magnetic Board With Letters**

S **Post Office Kit**

T **Make-Your-Own Big Book**

For more information about these materials, call 1-800-421-3018.

5

Zaner-Bloser's CONTINUOUS-STROKE manuscript alphabet

Aa Bb Cc Dd Ee Ff Gg
Oo Pp Qq Rr Ss Tt

Easier to Read

Our vertical manuscript alphabet is like the alphabet kids see every day inside and outside of the classroom. They see it in their school books, in important environmental print like road signs, and in books and cartoons they read for fun.

"[Slanted] manuscript is not only harder to learn than traditional [vertical] print, but it creates substantially more letter recognition errors and causes more letter confusion than does the traditional style."

–Debby Kuhl and Peter Dewitz in a paper presented at the 1994 meeting of the American Educational Research Association

Please, my friends, a moment of silence, as the flying Zucchinis attempt a twisting triple somersault.

CALIFORNIA LIN 216

STOP

Vertical manuscript is the alphabet we see every day.

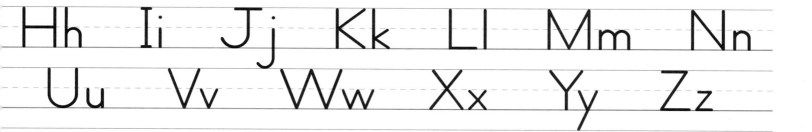

Easier to Write

Our vertical manuscript alphabet is written with continuous strokes—fewer pencil lifts—so there's a greater sense of flow in writing. And kids can write every letter once they learn four simple strokes that even kindergartners can manage.

Four simple strokes: circle, horizontal line, vertical line, slanted line

"The writing hand has to change direction more often when writing the [slanted] alphabet, do more retracing of lines, and make more strokes that occur later in children's development."

—Steve Graham in *Focus on Exceptional Children*, 1992

Many kids can already write their names when they start school (vertical manuscript).

Kirk

Why should they have to relearn them in another form (slanted manuscript)? With Zaner-Bloser, they don't have to.

Kirk

Easier to Teach

Our vertical manuscript alphabet is easy to teach because there's no reteaching involved. Children are already familiar with our letterforms—they've seen them in their environment and they've learned them at home.

"Before starting school, many children learn how to write traditional [vertical] manuscript letters from their parents or preschool teachers. Learning a special alphabet such as [slanted] means that these children will have to relearn many of the letters they can already write."

—Steve Graham in *Focus on Exceptional Children*, 1992

Vertical vs. *Slanted Manuscript*

What the research shows

Using a slanted alphabet has been a trend in handwriting instruction. It's actually not a new development—the first slanted alphabet was created in 1968. A sort of bridge between manuscript and cursive, this slanted alphabet used unconnected letterforms like the traditional vertical manuscript, but its letterforms were slanted like cursive.

It seemed like a good idea. This alphabet was to be easier to write than cursive, yet similar enough to cursive that children wouldn't learn two *completely* different alphabets. But after several years of use in some schools, research has uncovered some unfortunate findings.

Slanted manuscript can be difficult to write

Slanted manuscript was created to be similar to cursive, so it uses more complicated strokes such as small curves, and these strokes can be difficult for young children.

Vertical manuscript, on the other hand, is consistent with the development of young children. Each of its letters is formed with simple strokes—straight lines, circles, and slanted lines. One researcher found that the strokes used in vertical manuscript are the same as the shapes children use in their drawings (Farris, 1993). Because children are familiar with these shapes, they can identify and form the strokes with little difficulty.

Slanted manuscript can create problems with legibility

Legibility is an important goal in handwriting. Obviously, content should not be sacrificed for legibility, but what is handwriting if it cannot be read?

Educational researchers have tested the legibility of slanted manuscript and found that children writing vertical manuscript "performed significantly better" than those writing slanted manuscript. The writers of the slanted alphabet tended to make more misshapen letterforms, tended to extend their strokes above and below the guidelines, and had a difficult time keeping their letterforms consistent in size (Graham, 1992).

On the other hand, the vertical manuscript style of print has a lot of support in the area of research. Advertisers have known for years that italic type has a lower readability rate than vertical "roman" type. Research shows that in 30 minute readings, the italic style is read 4.9% slower than roman type (14–16 words per minute). This is why most literature, especially literature for early readers, is published using roman type.

Slanted manuscript can impair letter recognition

Educators have suspected that it would be beneficial for students to write and read the same style of alphabet. In other words, if children *read* vertical manuscript, they should also *write* vertical manuscript. Now it has been found that inconsistent alphabets may actually be detrimental to children's learning.

Researchers have found that slanted manuscript impairs the ability of some young children to recognize many letters. Some children who learn the slanted style alphabet find it difficult to recognize many of the traditional letterforms they see in books and environmental print. "[These children] consistently had difficulty identifying several letters, often making the same erroneous response to the same letter," the researchers reported. They concluded that slanted manuscript "creates substantially more letter recognition errors and causes more letter confusion than does the traditional style." (Kuhl & Dewitz, 1994).

Slanted manuscript does not help with transition

One of the benefits proposed by the creators of the slanted manuscript alphabet was that it made it easier for children to make the transition from manuscript to cursive writing. However, no difference in transition time has been found between the two styles of manuscript alphabets. In addition, the slanted style does not seem to enhance young children's production of cursive letters (Graham, 1992).

"…slanted manuscript letters cannot be recommended as a replacement for the traditional manuscript alphabet."

The slanted style of manuscript appeared to be a good idea. But educators should take a close look at what the research shows before adopting this style of alphabet. As one researcher has said, "Given the lack of supportive evidence and the practical problems involved in implementation, slanted manuscript letters cannot be recommended as a replacement for the traditional manuscript alphabet" (Graham, 1994).

Farris, P.J. (1993). Learning to write the ABC's: A comparison of D'Nealian and Zaner-Bloser handwriting styles. *Indiana Reading Quarterly, 25* (4), 26–33.

Graham, S. (1992). Issues in handwriting instruction. *Focus on Exceptional Children, 25* (2).

Graham, S. (1994, Winter). Are slanted manuscript alphabets superior to the traditional manuscript alphabet? *Childhood Education,* 91–95.

Kuhl, D. & Dewitz, P. (1994, April). The effect of handwriting style on alphabet recognition. Paper presented at the annual meeting of the American Educational Research Association, New Orleans, LA.

Emergent Writers

Children learn by doing. The more they experience and the more they practice, the more adept and confident they become. Children who are exposed to the printed word and have opportunities to see people reading and writing will themselves become stronger readers and build stronger writing ability. Many will grow up to be especially good writers, but all children benefit by mastering skills developed through writing and reading.

When very young children are given paper and writing instruments, they first make marks or dots, then they scribble, and eventually they draw. When you watch children play, you see that writing is important to them: They pretend to write letters and make menus; they take phone messages and create grocery lists. Whatever their level of emergent writing, these experiences help children develop writing and reading skills.

As children show signs of readiness, the teacher can provide guidance and instruction. This book helps teachers present formal and informal activities that foster the skills children need for writing and reading. It guides the teacher in using *Fun With Letters*, in which children learn to recognize and name letters and numerals. Children also learn the orientation of writing on a page and how to form letters and numerals correctly.

Much learning about letters and writing can take place in activity centers and through movement. This book concludes with games for circle time and for transitional moments. Some of the games can be set up as part of specific centers or used in direct instruction with small groups.

We want children to enjoy learning to write. They are constantly trying to make sense of the world—and writing gives them a giant key to that understanding.

Growing Up Writing

Young children develop handwriting readiness by drawing, scribbling, and writing.

Letter awareness begins when children find alphabet letters in their environment.

Your child learns a great deal during play because he thinks as he plays. Just as he plays with oral language ("silly, Billy, nilly, dilly"), he needs to play with written language. Further, he will enjoy playing with writing.

The principal concept behind writing awareness is that graphic symbols have meaning. Learning to read or write is immeasurably more difficult if children lack this basic knowledge about writing.

Beginning writers are eager writers. They like to show off their accomplishments. Bulletin board displays are especially appropriate for beginning writers. Many of their works are intended to be gifts. Their pictures contain words and their writing contains pictures.

For children, writing is a social event. In group settings, if a drawing/writing table is available, you will rarely see a child drawing or writing alone. Even at very young ages, children group themselves together to write and draw.

Peers provide a good support system for writing experiences.

The basic strokes for handwriting are circles and lines. As your child plays with tools, especially those for drawing and painting, he refines these basic strokes.

Excerpts from *Growing Up Writing* by Linda Leonard Lamme, Ph.D. Acropolis Books, Ltd., 1984, Washington, D.C.

Getting Started

Student Pages 5–8

Use these first four pages to help children understand the concept of a model. In this book, children will use a model as a reference first for recognizing shapes, then for recognizing and writing letters and numerals. As they engage in activities for each lesson, children will also use readiness skills.

Note: For your teaching convenience and so that family members can be informed of the purpose of the page, directions appear on each student page.

Before Children Use the Page

To begin each shape lesson, show children a cutout of the featured shape. Name it with children and ask them to look around and find examples of the shape in the classroom, such as a square windowpane, a round clock face, or a musical triangle.

Another way to present the model shape is to put cutouts around the classroom and ask children to find them as you provide clues; for example, say "I am a square and I am sitting on the piano bench."

After Children Complete the Page

Help children arrange themselves in the shape they have been focusing on. Begin with the whole group forming the target shape and then work with smaller groups. Children can stand or sit, facing inward or outward. You might call out two children's names and have them change places in the formation.

My ABC Book

Student Pages 9–12

Children will make take-home alphabet books to serve as a preview of uppercase alphabet letters that they will be learning to recognize and name.

Before Children Make the Book

Read aloud an ABC book from your collection. Tell children they can make an ABC book of their own. Show them a completed *My ABC Book* so they can visualize the final product.

After Children Make the Book

Read the completed book together. Have children take their books home to share with their families. Practice Master 119 is a letter home to accompany *My ABC Book*.

How to Make the Book

Help children carefully tear out the pages for *My ABC Book* along the perforations. Then show them how to fold along the fold line of both pages so that the title page and the **EFGH** page are on top. Have them tuck the part showing **EFGH** into the part that shows the title. Then staple each child's book along the spine.

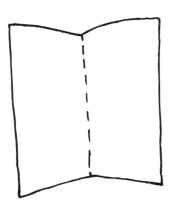

Naming Letters A–Z

Student Pages 13–38

Most educators recognize the correlation between success in letter recognition and later success in reading and writing. Use this section of the student book to help children name and recognize uppercase letters. Children will use a model as a reference when they do the activity on each page.

Directions: Point to and name the target letter with the children. Discuss the picture. Then have children find the **E**'s on the page. Ask them to color each space with the letter **E** the same color. Focus on **E** when you play one of the letter recognition games in the teacher guide. Use Practice Master 5.

17

Directions: Point to and name the target letter with the children. Discuss the picture. Then have children find the **R**'s on the page. Ask them to color each space with the letter **R** the same color. Focus on **R** when you play one of the letter recog-

Before Children Use the Page

Before you invite children to work through each letter page, present the target letter. Choose from the following suggestions.

• Sing "The Alphabet Song" with children. Then sing the song again. This time call attention to the target letter by asking children to stand up or clap when they hear the letter.

• Read an alphabet book. Call attention to the target letter. Invite children to use their hands to frame the letter on the page and to name it.

• Hide one or several letter cards marked with the target letter. Ask children to look for the hidden cards and to name the letter.

• Place the target letter card in a surprise box or bag. Ask children to guess the letter name before you display it.

• Distribute letter cards with a different letter to each child. Display the target letter card. Invite the child with the target letter to come up and match the letter.

• Display the target letter card. Invite children to find signs or labels in the classroom with that letter.

• Display the target letter card with a corresponding picture. Name the picture and talk about the first letter in the picture's name.

• Write the target letter on the chalkboard. Ask children with names that begin with the target letter to stand. Write each child's name on the board. Ask children to point to the target letter in each name.

29

After Children Complete the Page

Choose and play one of the letter recognition games that begin on page 24.

Use the Practice Master suggested on the student page to reinforce the lesson.

Help children understand that the letter they are focusing on represents a speech sound. Children will learn this easily through the use of the activities described in the Phonics Connection section on page 30.

• Write the target letter with a wet sponge on the chalkboard. Have children name the letter and chant the letter name until the letter disappears.

• Form the target letter with masking tape on the floor. Invite children to name the letter and to walk along its strokes.

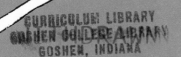

Learning Basic Strokes

Student Pages 39–56

As children progress from scribbles to strokes, they will learn the special vocabulary for handwriting. They will learn about left and right and directionality. They will practice handwriting strokes: pull down straight, slant, slide right, slide left, circle backward (left), and circle forward (right). Children will use the hidden letters page to review uppercase letters.

A Writing Center

This might be a good time to set up a handwriting center in your classroom with various kinds of paper and writing implements. Models of lines made from a variety of materials such as yarn, string, or glitter would reinforce the basic handwriting strokes you are teaching. Children would enjoy helping you make them and could use them as models when they write independently.

Before Children Write

In this section, children make the strokes they will use in writing. It is a time for them to learn how to hold their pencils and how to position their papers for handwriting ease.

Right-handed writers should keep the paper straight and pull vertical lines toward the middle of the body. Left-handed writers should slant the paper slightly and pull vertical lines toward the left elbow.

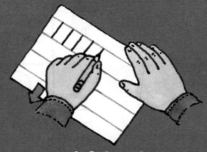

left hand

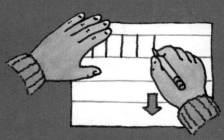

right hand

PENCIL POSITION

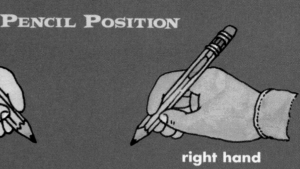

left hand

right hand

Children who have difficulty using the traditional position may prefer the alternate method of holding the pencil between the first two fingers.

Remember start at the ●. Stop at the ●.

Write some slant lines. We're going to help you write.

Play a "Stop and Go" game and remind children that a green dot signals where to start writing a line and a red dot signals where to stop. Finger tracing the model lines may help them visualize the line they will write between the slant lines. Use Practice Masters 28 and 29.

51

Start at the ●. Stop at the ●.

Write some pull down straight lines.

50

Before children use this page you might play "Stop and Go" by using a green and a red dot to signal children when to walk around the room and when to stop. Explain that green often signals go and red often signals stop. Model writing lines that start at a green dot and stop at a red dot before children write. Use Practice Master 27.

Which Hand?

If a child is definitely left-handed, teach him or her to write with that hand. If you have questions about hand dominance, conduct a simple test. Observe each child as he or she plays with a hand puppet, puts pegs in a pegboard, throws a ball, holds a spoon, and cuts with scissors. Keep a tally of which hand is used for each task. If a child is truly ambidextrous, it is probably best to train the right hand.

The Left-Handed Child

- Discourage the hooked-wrist writing position by modeling correct paper placement for the left-hander (see diagram).
- Allow the left-hander to practice free, full arm movement by writing on the chalkboard.
- Show the left-hander how to hold the pencil a little higher than the right-hander (well above the raw wood).
- Group left-handers together occasionally for instruction and reinforcement.

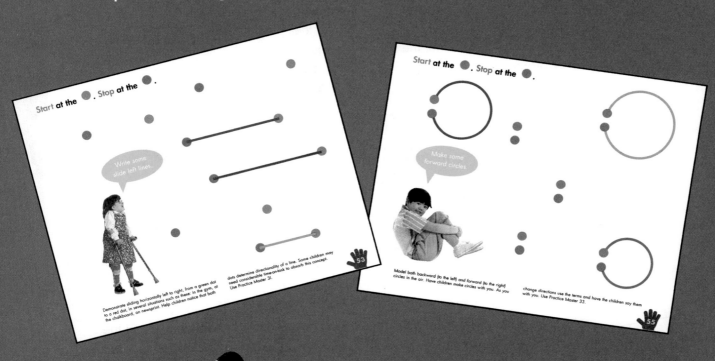

After Children Write

Play one of the handwriting games from pages 31 and 32. Use the Practice Master suggested on the student page.

My Alphabet Museum

Student Pages 57–62

Children will make take-home alphabet books to serve as a preview of lowercase alphabet letters that they will be learning to recognize and name.

Before Children Make the Book

Read aloud an ABC book from your collection. Tell children they can make an ABC book of their own. So they can visualize the final product, show them a completed *My Alphabet Museum*. Explain that the letters they already know are upper-case letters and that the new letters are lowercase letters.

After Children Make the Book

Read the book together. Ask children to take their books home to share with their families. Practice Master 120 is a letter home to accompany *My Alphabet Museum*.

How to Make the Book

Help children carefully tear out the pages for *My Alphabet Museum* along the perforations. Show them how to fold along the fold lines of the pages so that the title page, the **Dd** and **Ee** page, and the **Hh**, **Ii**, and **Jj** page are on top. Have them tuck the page showing **Dd** and **Ee** into the part that shows the title. Then have them tuck in the page showing **Hh**, **Ii**, and **Jj** to complete the book. Staple each child's book along the spine. Help children name and complete a picture for each letter.

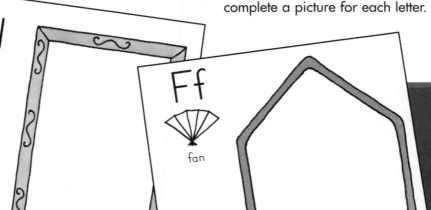

Naming and Writing Letter Pairs

Student Pages 63–114

Use this section to help children name and write uppercase and lowercase letters. The letter pairs are grouped by common strokes of the uppercase letters. Two pages are provided for each letter pair. Each writing page has a corresponding activity page. Use these pages to introduce the letters and to provide writing practice.

Before Children Write Letters

Model writing the target letters. Write the uppercase letter on guidelines on the chalkboard as you say the stroke descriptions on the bottom of the student page. Then have children model the writing with you, using one of the following suggestions.

• Model writing the target letter in the air as you say the stroke descriptions. Ask children to echo the stroke descriptions as they write in the air with you.

• Have groups of children come to the chalkboard, dip their index fingers in a container of water, and write the target letter on the board. Ask children to say the stroke descriptions with you as they write.

• Invite some children to dip a small sponge in water and use it to write the target letter on the chalkboard while the others say the stroke descriptions with you.

• Invite children to use an index finger to write the target letter on their desks. Ask them to say the stroke descriptions with you as they write.

• Model writing the target letter on sandpaper. Pair children and have them take turns writing and saying the stroke descriptions.

Repeat the procedure for the lowercase letter.

After Children Write Letters

Play any of the following games, using the pictures on the page.

• Ask children to point to each picture as you name it. Then ask them to hide one picture with their hand. Tell them that they may "peek" at their picture at any time. Then say, "Raise your hand if you hid the (picture word)." Continue until all the pictures are named.

• Ask children to point to each picture as you name it. Have them find the word that labels each picture as you read it.

• Ask children to point to the target letter as you say each picture word. Invite them to take turns naming each picture. Then ask them to draw a line under the target letter that begins the word.

• Ask children to listen and to find a specific word. Use statements such as these: "I am thinking of a word that begins with **b** and ends with **r**." "I am thinking of a word that begins with **b** and ends with **y**."

• Ask children to point to each picture as you name it. To focus attention on recognizing letters, ask a volunteer to choose one picture word

and to name all the letters. Then ask if anyone can guess which word was chosen.

• Give children opportunities to write target letters on laminated cards or slates. This gives children time on task without being concerned with making mistakes.

You might also choose and play one of the letter recognition games or Phonics Connection activities that begin on page 24. Use the Practice Masters suggested on the student page to reinforce the lesson.

Student Pages 63–114

Before Children Use the Page

Before you invite children to use the activity page, review the pair of target letters. Choose from the following suggestions.

• Write the uppercase and lowercase target letters on the chalkboard. Have volunteers name and trace each letter.

• Read an alphabet book aloud. Call attention to the target letters. Invite children to frame the letter or letters on the page, name them, and identify them as uppercase or lowercase letters.

• Display the uppercase and lowercase target letters. Invite children to find signs or labels in the classroom with the letters.

• Distribute a lowercase letter card to each child. Be sure several cards have the target letter. Display the uppercase target letter card. Invite children who have the corresponding lowercase letter to come up and match the letters.

• Write the uppercase target letter on the chalkboard. Invite children to write the matching lowercase letter next to it.

• Prepare two sets of sign boards, half with the uppercase target letters and half with the lowercase target letters. Have children put on the signs and then find their partners.

• On a bulletin board, place a column of uppercase target letters and a column of lowercase target letters in a different order. Invite children to use yarn to match the letters.

After Children Complete the Page

Choose and play one of the letter recognition games that begin on page 24. Use the Practice Master suggested on the student page to reinforce the lesson.

To reinforce children's understanding that the letter they are focusing on represents a speech sound, do one of the activities in the Phonics Connection section on page 30.

Naming and Writing Numerals

You may wish to coordinate these pages with your mathematics program, using them at the point of initial teaching or as a review.

Directions: Help children identify numerals **5** and **6**. Have them touch and count the objects in each group. Ask children to draw a line around the group of five.

Stroke Descriptions **5:** Pull down straight. Circle forward (right). Lift. Slide right. **6:** Curve down. Curve up and around to close the circle. Use Practice Master 115.

117

Directions: Explain that the numerals **1–10** are hidden in this picture. Help children find **1** and **2**. Ask them to draw a line around each numeral in the picture. Help children find all the numerals before they color the picture.

121

Before Children Use the Page

You might want to begin with having the children say a rhyme, such as:

1, 2, 3, 4, 5

I caught a fish alive.

6, 7, 8, 9, 10

I put it back again.

Prepare cards for the numerals 1–10 and show each numeral as you say its name in the rhyme. Then give a numeral card to a child. Have the children say the rhyme again with you and ask the child with the numeral card to hold it up when the numeral's name is said. When two numerals are in the lesson, add a second card as the game catches on.

After Children Complete the Page

Ask children to fold a paper in two. Say a numeral they have written and ask them to write it on one part. Then ask them to write another numeral on the other part. Suggest that they look at the first numeral they wrote and draw that many dots near it. Do the same for the second numeral. After they have learned to write several numerals, you might like to tally which one the most children chose to write and declare it the numeral of the day.

Use the Practice Master suggested on the student page to reinforce the lesson.

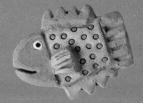
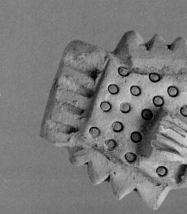

Me, Myself, and I

Student Pages 123–128
You may wish to complete the pages with the children or send the books home for children to complete with family members.

Before Children Make the Book

Help children make the books to take home. Give them a few minutes to look at the pages and to make comments about what they see. Read the directions with the children and discuss what they will do to complete their books.

After Children Make the Book

If children have made their book in school, you may want to have them share it with a buddy. Have them complete the letter (Practice Master 121) to accompany their take-home book.

This is what I like about school.

This is what I like f

Here are lette

Fun and Games

Letter Recognition

The following games can be adapted for most letters in the alphabet. Some of these games can be played at transitional moments or when you have an extra five minutes. Several are appropriate for ongoing use in play centers in the classroom.

We're Going on a Letter Hunt

What You Need:

Letters cut from magazines
Letters written on index cards

What You Do:

Take children around the classroom on a scavenger hunt for a single letter, such as **B**. Before going on this excursion, cut the letter out of magazines or write the letter several times on index cards. Hide the letters in fairly obvious places around the classroom. You might want to start the game with the chant:

We're going on a letter hunt.
We're going to find some **B**'s (or another letter).
Are you ready?
Let's go!

Have children walk in small groups looking for the letters. You may want to repeat the chant as children search. You can play this game in different locations around the school. (visual, auditory, kinesthetic)

Mystery Letter Collages

What You Need:

Paper for mural
Magazines and newspapers
Scissors
Glue

What You Do:

Write a letter on a large piece of mural paper and roll the paper into a tube. Ask children to guess which letter you wrote, and then unroll the paper. Name the letter on the paper with the children. Invite them to cut the letter out of magazines and newspapers. Have them glue the letters onto the paper to create a mural of a particular letter. (visual, kinesthetic)

24

Grocery Store

What You Need:

Brown paper bags
Empty boxes and food containers wrapped in plain paper
Markers

What You Do:

Print letters on the outside of brown paper bags. Write single letters on the outside of the empty food containers. Encourage children to sort the groceries into the matching letter bags. This game is fun in the dramatic play area. (visual, kinesthetic)

Letter Cards

What You Need:

Construction paper cut into circles
Markers

What You Do:

Make two sets of letter cards using the construction paper. Print two cards for each letter. Lay one set in a row on the floor. Scramble the second set and lay them in a row beside the first set. Invite children to rearrange the second set to match the first set. Vary this game by changing the shape of the letter cards or the letters used in the game. (visual, kinesthetic)

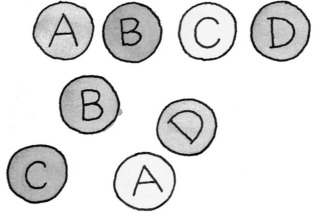

Post Office

What You Need:

Shoe boxes
Index cards with a different letter printed on each one
Envelopes with a letter printed on each one

What You Do:

Make pretend mailboxes by attaching the index cards to the shoe boxes. Invite children to deliver the mail by sorting the envelopes into the matching shoe boxes. (visual, kinesthetic)

Parachute Play

What You Need:

Parachute or a large fitted sheet
Index cards with a letter printed on each one

What You Do:

Spread out the parachute and place the index cards in the center of it. Have children march in a circle, raising and lowering the edges of the parachute. As children walk, encourage them to sing "The Alphabet Song." When the song ends, lower the parachute and invite children to identify the letters on the parachute that are faceup. (visual, auditory, kinesthetic)

Sponge Painting

What You Need:

Paper
Paint
Sponges cut into letter shapes

What You Do:

Near the art table, display letter cards that correspond to the sponge letters. Invite children to make letters by dipping the sponge letters into paint and printing with them. (visual, kinesthetic)

Come Back to the Circle

What You Need:

Index cards with letters printed on them
Construction paper sheets with a large letter printed on each one

What You Do:

Give each child an index card with a letter printed on it. Then have children scatter to different parts of the classroom. Hold up a large construction paper letter for the children to see. Have the child who is holding the matching index card identify the letter and return to the circle area. (visual)

Find the Secret Message

What You Need:

Chart paper or chalkboard
Markers or chalk

What You Do:

At the end of the day, draw children's attention back to your daily message chart. Choose a letter and ask one child to find and mark it on the chart. Invite individual children to find that letter in other words on the chart. (visual)

Concentration

What You Need:

Two sets of index cards with letters on them

What You Do:

Encourage small groups of children to play this memory game. Mix the two sets of letter cards. Place them face-down in several rows. Invite children to take turns turning over two cards to make a match. If they turn over two like cards, they keep the pair. If the two cards don't match, the cards are turned over and the next player chooses. (visual, kinesthetic)

Letter Bracelets

What You Need:

Yarn
Markers
Hole puncher
Tagboard shapes

What You Do:

Write different letters on tagboard shapes, punch a hole in each shape, and put each shape on a piece of yarn to make several bracelets. Distribute the bracelets to children to wear for the day. During the school day, give instructions, such as "Will the children wearing the letter **G** get their coats?" or "All children whose bracelets have the letter **R** should come pick out a book now." (visual, auditory)

Musical Alphabet

What You Need:

Index cards with letters printed on them

What You Do:

Give each child a card with a letter printed on it. Have children hold the cards on their laps as they sing this adaptation of a popular song:

If you have a **J** in your lap, give a clap.
If you have a **J** in your lap, give a clap.
If you have a **J** in your lap, don't be shy, give a clap.
If you have a **J** in your lap, give a clap!

You may wish to have children make different motions for each letter. (visual, auditory, kinesthetic)

What Does It Look Like?

What You Need:

Chart paper
Markers

What You Do:

Write a letter on a piece of paper and display it in a place where children can easily see it. Ask children to describe the way the letter looks. For example, an **M** could be described as having three points, having four lines, looking like cat's ears, and so on. (auditory, visual)

Glue Stick Letters

What You Need:

Tagboard or cardboard
Markers
Glue sticks
Buttons, beans, small pieces of paper

What You Do:

Give each child a piece of tagboard with a letter written on it. Tell children to trace the letter with a glue stick. Have them attach small objects, such as buttons, beans, or small pieces of paper. (kinesthetic)

Body Shape Letters

What You Do:
Have children play this game in small groups. Whisper the name of a letter to one group. Have the children in that group use their bodies to form the letter. Encourage them to work as a team. Some children might lie on the floor to make the shape as other children help direct the pose. Encourage each group to take a turn at forming letters. (visual, kinesthetic)

Pretzel Letters

What You Need:
2 packages dry yeast
1/2 cup warm water
2 Tbs. sugar
1 tsp. salt
4 cups flour
1 egg, beaten
Measuring cups and spoons
Mixing bowl
Floured board
Cookie sheet

What You Do:
Use this recipe and invite children to create letter-shaped pretzels!
1. Preheat oven to 425° F.
2. Mix warm water and yeast.
3. Add the sugar, salt, and flour.
4. Knead the mixture on a floured board.
5. Form pieces of dough into letter shapes and lay them on the cookie sheet.
6. Brush with beaten egg.
7. Bake for about 12–15 minutes.
(kinesthetic, visual)

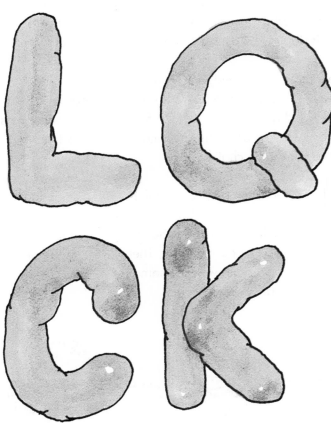

Phonics Connection

The following activity can be used to help children develop their understanding of sound-symbol correspondence. Use it to present the sounds of letters.

The Sounds of Letters

What You Need:
Anthologies of children's songs
Anthologies of children's poems

What You Do:
With children, say a rhyme or sing a song that contains the target letter. Choose your own favorites or select from the titles listed. After children become familiar with the verse, isolate one word that begins with the target sound.

For example, when studying **Tt**, recite "The Little Turtle" by Vachel Lindsay. Write *turtle* on the chalkboard. Say "turtle," and ask children to listen for the sound that begins the word. Have them name the letter that begins the word, and write it on the chalkboard.

Ask children to listen as you say other words, some that begin like *turtle* and some that do not. Ask children to tap their shoulders if the word they hear begins like *turtle*. Have them trace **T** or **t** in the air. Then ask them to name other words that begin with the same sound as *turtle*. (auditory, visual, kinesthetic)

Songs and Poems

A: "Apples, Peaches, Pears, and Plums"

B: "Bingo"

C: "Who Took the Cookie From the Cookie Jar?"

D: "Diddle, Diddle, Dumpling"

E: "Eletelephony"

F: "Five Little Pumpkins"

G: "Good Morning to You"

H: "If You're Happy and You Know It"

I: "Bluebird in My Window"

J: "Jack and Jill"

K: "Three Little Kittens"

L: "Ladybug, Ladybug"

M: "Monkey See and Do"

N: "The Little Nut Tree"

O: "Polly Put the Kettle On," "On Top of Old Smoky"

P: "Pop Goes the Weasel"

Q: "Six Little Ducks"

R: "Rain, Rain Go Away"

S: "Sing a Song of Sixpence"

T: "The Little Turtle"

U: "Sleeping Outdoors," "The Umbrella Brigade"

V: "The Cat Came Back"

W: "It's a Small World"

X: "Little Boxes"

Y: "Yankee Doodle"

Z: "Going to the Zoo"

Handwriting Strokes

The following games encourage children to use their knowledge of spatial orientation and of how to form letters. These games can be adapted for most letters in the alphabet.

Sand Writing

What You Need:
A baking pan or cookie sheet
Sand or cornmeal
Index cards with letters on them

What You Do:
Fill the tray with sand or other fine-grain material. Encourage children to make lines and circles in the sand. Then have individual children look at the letter on each index card and write that letter in the sand. (kinesthetic, visual)

Sewing Cards

What You Need:
Hole punches
Tagboard
Yarn

What You Do:

Invite children to help you make a set of sewing cards. This is an enjoyable way to help develop tactile skills. Children may simply punch random holes in the tagboard while you punch out letters of the alphabet. Encourage children to sew the cards, using different colors of yarn. (kinesthetic, visual)

Clay Writing

What You Need:
Plasticene
Dull primary pencils
Index cards with letters printed on them

What You Do:
Ask children to press and pound pieces of plasticene. Have them use the dull point of a pencil to make straight lines and circle lines. They may want to refer to the letter cards as they try to write letters. (kinesthetic)

Extra! Extra!

What You Need:

Newspaper sheets

What You Do:

Distribute a sheet of newspaper to each child. Give directions such as these:

> Hold up the newspaper with your right hand.
> Hold up the newspaper with your left hand.
> Put the newspaper under your right foot.
> Put the newspaper under your left foot.
> Stand at the top of your paper.
> Jump on the middle of your paper.
> Tiptoe along the bottom of your paper.

(auditory, kinesthetic)

Chalkboard, Chalk, and Water

What You Need:

Paintbrushes
Water bucket
Index cards with letters printed on them

What You Do:

Invite several children to dip paintbrushes in water and make water marks on the chalkboard. Use the stroke descriptions, such as "pull down straight," or "slant left," to encourage children to develop proper writing strokes. (visual, kinesthetic, auditory)

Potato Prints

What You Need:

Potatoes, cut in half
Paint
Dull primary pencils
Paper

What You Do:

Children can create interesting designs with the basic strokes of handwriting. Gouge out lines on cut potatoes. Have children dip their potatoes in paint and print with them on paper. Remember to use basic stroke terminology, such as "Show a pull down straight stroke" or "You made three slant left strokes." (visual, kinesthetic)

Simon Says

What You Do:

Play the traditional game of "Simon Says," but use words that relate to writing. Directions, such as "Simon says slide right; Simon says slide left; circle forward" help children understand the terms they will use as they learn to write. (kinesthetic, auditory)

Hokey-Pokey

What You Do:

Try this adaptation of a favorite circle game to help children practice directionality and basic handwriting strokes. With children, sing the words and act out the movements directed in each line.

> Put your right hand in.
> Put your right hand out.
> Put your right hand in.
> And you shake it all about.
> You slide to the right
> And you slide to the left
> And that's how we play our game!

(auditory, kinesthetic)